Orange Line 2

Vokabellernheft

Herausgeber: Dr. Frank Haß

Ernst Klett Verlag
Stuttgart • Leipzig

Liebe Schülerin, lieber Schüler,

mit diesem Vokabellernheft im praktischen Taschenformat kannst du überall deine Wörter lernen, wiederholen und nachschlagen.
In den Wortlisten kannst du Wörter und Wendungen, die dir schwierig vorkommen, mit Textmarker oder Bleistift markieren, um sie dann immer wieder durchzugehen.
Auch die vielen Übungen nach jeder Unit unterstützen dich bei der Wiederholung. So kannst du dich prima auf Vokabeltests vorbereiten.

In den Übungen, die mit diesem Zeichen ● gekennzeichnet sind, übst du die blau gedruckten Wörter.

Hinter jedem Wort ist die Lautschrift (z. B. [fæn'tæstɪk] für *fantastic*) angegeben. Diese hilft dir, wenn du nicht weißt, wie du das Wort aussprechen sollst.
Hilfreiche Hinweise zum Umgang mit den Lautschriftzeichen findest du **in deinem Englischbuch** auf Seite 187 und ab Seite 240 am unteren Rand aller *Dictionary*-Seiten.

Viel Erfolg beim Vokabellernen!

Unit 1 Friends

Way in

p. 8	**I'm fine.** [ˌaɪm 'faɪn]	Mir geht es gut.
p. 9	**Jamaica** [dʒə'meɪkə]	Jamaika
	aunt [ɑ:nt]	Tante
	fantastic [fæn'tæstɪk]	fantastisch; großartig
	to **visit** ['vɪzɪt]	besuchen
	grandparents *(pl)* ['grænˌpeərənts]	Großeltern
p. 8	to **ask about** ['ɑ:sk‿əˌbaʊt]	sich erkundigen nach; fragen nach
	to **talk about** ['tɔ:k‿əˌbaʊt]	sprechen über
p. 9	**hat** [hæt]	Hut

Station 1

Holiday activities

to **start a band** [ˌstɑ:t‿ə 'bænd]	eine Band gründen
to **take photos** [ˌteɪk 'fəʊtəʊz]	fotografieren; Fotos machen
to **go shopping** [ˌgəʊ 'ʃɒpɪŋ]	einkaufen gehen
to **visit a museum** [ˌvɪzɪt‿ə mju:'zi:əm]	ein Museum besuchen
to **stay in a hotel** [ˌsteɪ ɪn‿ə həʊ'tel]	in einem Hotel übernachten
to **pack a suitcase** [ˌpæk‿ə 'su:tkeɪs]	einen Koffer packen
to **hang (around)** [ˌhæŋ‿ə'raʊnd], **hung** [hʌŋ]	(herum)hängen
to **climb a mountain** [ˌklaɪm‿ə 'maʊntɪn]	einen Berg besteigen

to buy a souvenir [ˌbaɪ ə suːvnˈɪə]	ein Souvenir kaufen
to sunbathe on the beach [ˌsʌnbeɪð ɒn ðə ˈbiːtʃ]	sonnenbaden am Strand
to fly to another country [ˌflaɪ tʊ əˌnʌðə ˈkʌntri]	in ein anderes Land fliegen

p. 10	**summer** [ˈsʌmə]	Sommer
	parents *(pl)* [ˈpeərnts]	Eltern
	to **stay** [steɪ]	übernachten; bleiben
	city [ˈsɪti]	Stadt; Großstadt
	cousin [ˈkʌzn]	Cousin; Cousine
	sang [sæŋ]	simple past von *to sing* (singen)
	before [bɪˈfɔː]	bevor
	to **get married** [ˌget ˈmærɪd]	heiraten
	wedding [ˈwedɪŋ]	Hochzeit
	end [end]	Ende; Schluss
	ate [eɪt]	simple past von *to eat* (essen)
	cricket [ˈkrɪkɪt]	Kricket
	ball [bɔːl]	Ball
	grandfather [ˈgrænˌfaːðə]	Großvater
	well [wel]	gut
	to **feel** [fiːl], **felt** [felt]	(sich) fühlen
	It's Holly's turn. [ɪts ˈhɒliz ˌtɜːn]	Holly ist dran.
	everyone [ˈevriwʌn]	*hier:* zusammen
p. 13	**took** [tʊk]	simple past von *to take* (nehmen)

Station 2

Feelings

surprised [sə'praɪzd]	überrascht
worried ['wʌrid]	beunruhigt; besorgt
angry ['æŋgri]	wütend; zornig; verärgert; böse
excited [ɪk'saɪtɪd]	aufgeregt; begeistert
unhappy [ʌn'hæpi]	unglücklich
afraid [ə'freɪd]	ängstlich
relaxed [rɪ'lækst]	entspannt; locker; gelassen
glad [glæd]	froh
confused [kən'fju:zd]	verwirrt; wirr
nervous ['nɜ:vəs]	nervös; aufgeregt
jealous ['dʒeləs]	eifersüchtig; neidisch

p. 14	**argument** ['ɑ:gjəmənt]	Auseinandersetzung; Streit
	the blue one [ðə 'blu:‿wʌn]	der blaue
	to **borrow** ['bɒrəʊ]	ausleihen
	to **bring** [brɪŋ], **brought** [brɔ:t]	bringen; mitbringen
	to **understand** [ˌʌndə'stænd], **understood** [ˌʌndə'stʊd]	verstehen
	to **lose** [lu:z], **lost** [lɒst]	verlieren
	to **have to** ['hæv tə], **had to** ['hæd tə]	müssen
	mine [maɪn]	meins; meine
	when [wen]	wenn; als
	to **look** [lʊk]	aussehen; sehen
	hers [hɜ:z]	ihre
	That's what happened. [ˌðæts wɒt 'hæpnd]	Das ist passiert.
	to **happen** ['hæpn]	geschehen; passieren
	to **lend** [lend], **lent** [lent]	leihen; verleihen

	so [səʊ]	so
	the same [ðə 'seɪm]	derselbe; gleich
	as [æz]	wie
	Never mind. [ˌnevə 'maɪnd]	Macht nichts.; Schon gut.; Mach dir nichts draus.
	his [hɪz]	seins; seiner
p. 15	**club** [klʌb]	Klub; Verein
	little ['lɪtl]	klein
	phone [fəʊn]	Telefon
	What's wrong? [ˌwɒts 'rɒŋ]	Was ist los?; Was stimmt nicht?
	to **use** [ju:z]	benutzen; verwenden
	It doesn't matter. [ɪt ˌdʌznt 'mætə]	Es ist egal.
	Don't worry. [ˌdəʊnt 'wʌri]	Mach dir keine Sorgen.
p. 16	**concert** ['kɒnsət]	Konzert
	again [ə'gen]	wieder; noch einmal

Reading corner

p. 18	**lucky day** [ˌlʌki 'deɪ]	Glückstag
	on the bus [ˌɒn ðə 'bʌs]	im Bus
	to **get** [get], **got** [gɒt]	holen
	takeaway ['teɪkəweɪ]	zum Mitnehmen
	tonight [tə'naɪt]	heute Abend; heute Nacht
	tuna ['tju:nə]	Thunfisch
	I'm playing [aɪm 'pleɪɪŋ]	ich spiele gerade
	score [skɔ:]	Punktestand
	eye [aɪ]	Auge
	everything ['evriθɪŋ]	alles
	out of ['aʊt‿əv]	aus … heraus
	stop [stɒp]	Haltestelle; Halt
	tomorrow [tə'mɒrəʊ]	morgen
	to **rush down** [rʌʃ 'daʊn]	hinuntereilen
	stairs *(pl)* [steəz]	Treppe
	to **get off** [ˌget‿'ɒf], **got off** [ˌgɒt‿'ɒf]	aussteigen

	to **finish** ['fɪnɪʃ]	beenden; enden; aufhören
	pocket ['pɒkɪt]	Tasche; Hosentasche
	I must have forgotten it. [aɪ ˌmʌst hæv fə'gɒtn‿ɪt]	Ich muss es vergessen haben.
	to **look up** [ˌlʊk‿'ʌp]	aufschauen; nachschauen
	not ... any more [ˌnɒt eni 'mɔː]	nicht mehr
	to **phone** [fəʊn]	anrufen; telefonieren
	company ['kʌmpəni]	Gesellschaft; Firma
	to **enjoy** [ɪn'dʒɔɪ]	genießen
	dinner ['dɪnə]	Abendessen
	not at all [ˌnɒt‿ət‿'ɔːl]	überhaupt nicht; gar nicht
	that night [ˌðæt 'naɪt]	an jenem Abend; in jener Nacht
	careful ['keəfl]	vorsichtig; sorgfältig
	suddenly ['sʌdnli]	plötzlich; auf einmal
	rang [ræŋ]	simple past von *to ring* (klingeln)
	to **shout** [ʃaʊt]	schreien; rufen
	hall [hɔːl]	Flur; Diele; Korridor
	gave [geɪv]	simple past von *to give* (geben)
p. 19	**That's what friends are for!** [ˌðæts wɒt ˌfrendz‿ɑː 'fɔː]	Dafür sind Freunde da!
	best ever score [best ˌevə 'skɔː]	das beste Ergebnis

Film corner

p. 21	**between** [bɪ'twiːn]	zwischen
	experiment [ɪk'sperɪmənt]	Versuch
	have you got [ˌhæv juː 'gɒt]	hast du
	comic ['kɒmɪk]	Comic(heft)
	to **ruin** ['ruːɪn]	ruinieren; zerstören
	to **break** [breɪk], **broke** [brəʊk]	brechen; zerbrechen
	on purpose [ɒn 'pɜːpəs]	absichtlich
	true [truː]	wahr
	Stop it! ['stɒp‿ɪt]	Hör(t) auf!

	to **be right** [biː 'raɪt]	recht haben
	all right [ˌɔːl 'raɪt]	in Ordnung; alles klar

Viewing skills

p. 26	**How to …** ['haʊ tə]	Wie man …
	polite [pə'laɪt]	höflich
	scene [siːn]	Szene
p. 27	to **walk** [wɔːk]	laufen
	to **show** [ʃəʊ]	zeigen
	to **get to know** [ˌget tə 'nəʊ]	kennen lernen
	What to … ['wɒt tə]	Was man …
	situation [ˌsɪtju'eɪʃn]	Situation
	best [best]	beste
	queue [kjuː]	Warteschlange
	escalator ['eskəleɪtə]	Rolltreppe
	to **wake up** [ˌweɪk‿'ʌp], **woke up** [ˌwəʊk‿'ʌp]	aufwachen
	to **say sorry** [ˌseɪ 'sɒri]	sich entschuldigen

Wenn du ein neues Wort lernst, überlege dir, ob du Wörter zum gleichen Thema kennst, z.B.:

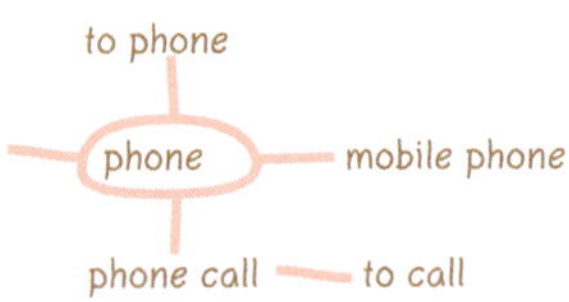

1 Find the words and write them down.

X	S	E	L	A	U	N	T	R
O	Z	S	A	B	W	I	V	S
F	A	N	T	A	S	T	I	C
P	R	E	S	E	N	T	S	H
D	A	R	Q	C	Y	L	I	A
	C	R	I	C	K	E	T	T

1. Tante ______________ 4. Hut ______________

2. großartig ______________ 5. Geschenk ______________

3. besuchen ______________ 6. Kricket ______________

2 Make sentences.

1. In the summer my cousins a) hotel.
2. We went to their b) museum.
3. We stayed in a c) shopping.
4. My dad took lots of d) wedding.
5. My sister went e) got married.
6. We all visited a f) photos.

3 Complete the sentences with family words.

1. Your mum and dad are your ______________ .
2. Your parents' parents are your ______________ .
3. Your dad's brother is your ______________ .
4. Your mum's father is your ______________ .
5. Your aunt's daughters are your ______________ .

4 Find the words.

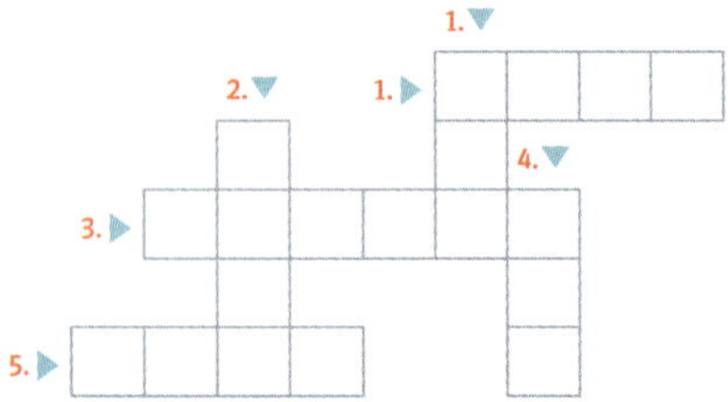

▶ 1. a big town
3. not after
5. You play tennis with this.

▼ 1. You go places in this.
2. “gut” in English
4. The last page is at the ….

5 Find the words and write them.

dissurpre | wordrie | ganry
detexci | pyhaunp | hygrun

1. They aren’t so good at cricket. I’m ____________ they won.
2. It’s my birthday next week. I’m really ____________ .
3. My brother has a test tomorrow. He’s ____________ about it.
4. My sister broke the chair and my dad is ____________ with her now.
5. We’re very ____________ because we can’t find our cat.
6. Let’s have a sandwich. I’m so ____________ .

6 Complete the dialogues.

Olivia: Holly! Is this ________ hat?

Holly: No, it's not ________ . Isn't it Lucy's?

Olivia: No, it isn't ________ . It's very big. Is it ________ , Jay?

Jay: No, it isn't ________ hat, but I like it. Can I …?

Olivia: No, you can't, Jay. Maybe there's a name in it.

Holly: Oh yes … here: It says "Luke". Sorry, Jay, it's ________ .

7 Write the words.

1. 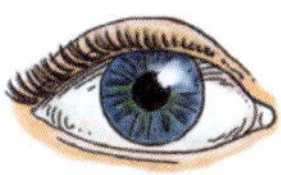

____

2. 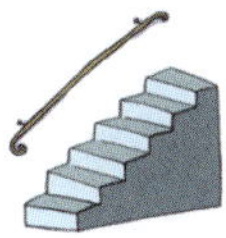

____

3. 

____

4. 

____

5. 

____

6. 

____

8 Write the words in English.

1. morgen ________
2. heute Abend ________
3. Konzert ________
4. Firma ________
5. Punktestand ________
6. Abendessen ________
7. plötzlich ________
8. Hosentasche ________

9 Find and write the verbs. Complete the table.

E	N	J	O	Y	E	D	R	B	T
A	W	Q	F	E	L	T	Y	R	C
L	B	O	R	R	O	W	G	I	K
U	N	D	E	R	S	T	A	N	D
S	H	A	P	P	E	N	V	G	D
A	F	G	E	T	E	L	E	N	T

German	English infinitive	Simple past
1. genießen		
2. ausleihen		
3. bringen		
4. geben		
5. fühlen		
6. geschehen		
7. verleihen		
8. verlieren		
9. verstehen		
10. holen		

10 Find the phrases. Complete the dialogues.

Haveyougotonpurposestopitisrightallright

1. Why did you do that? – I didn't do it ______________ .
2. He says it's a great comic. – Yes, he ______________ .
3. ______________ time for lunch? – Yes, but let's get a takeaway.
4. I'm sorry I lost your pencil. – It's ______________ .
5. Hey, ______________ . – Oh, I'm sorry.

11 Find the words.

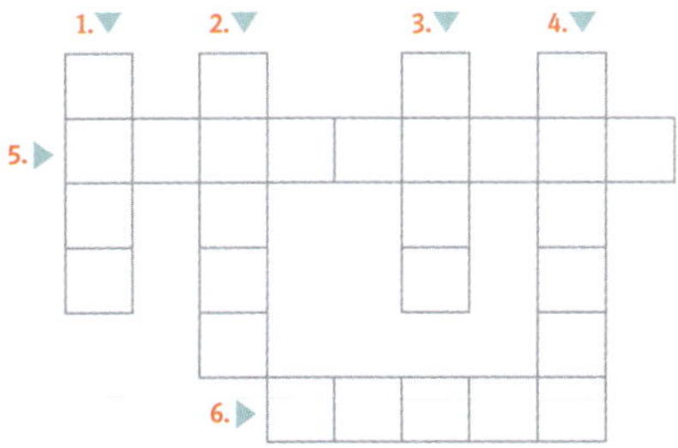

▼ 1. good, better, …
2. The first … of the film is at our school.
3. I usually … up at 7 o'clock.
4. Teacher: Always be … and don't shout.

▶ 5. You can go up on an … .
6. In England people stand in a … at a bus stop.

●12 Find the words.

1. My brother is __________ of mice.
2. My dad's cool. He's always __________ about things.
3. We had an argument. I'm __________ we're friends again.
4. We have a test tomorrow. I'm __________ about it.
5. Ken likes me, but he likes my sister more. I'm __________ .
6. We're __________ . What do we have to do?

●13 Find the activities and make sentences.

1. 
2. 

3. 

______________ ______________ ______________

4. 
5. 
6. 

______________ ______________ ______________

1. On holiday I often hang	a) on the beach.
2. But sometimes we go on	b) down to the sea.
3. We love to sunbathe	c) a mountain and take photos.
4. It often gets hot so I rush	d) a trip to the sea.
5. Sometimes we fly	e) around with friends.
6. I love to climb	f) to another country.

Unit 2 Stars!

Way in

p. 28	**star** [stɑ:]	Star
	player ['pleɪə]	Spieler; Spielerin
	crowd [kraʊd]	Menschenmenge
	prize [praɪz]	Preis
	stage [steɪdʒ]	Bühne
	to **organize** ['ɔ:gənaɪz]	organisieren
	jumble sale ['dʒʌmbl ˌseɪl]	Flohmarkt
	to **be afraid** [bi: ə'freɪd]	sich fürchten; Angst haben
	others ['ʌðəz]	anderen
	You can do it! [ˌju: kæn 'du ɪt]	Du schaffst es!
p. 29	to **draw** [drɔ:], **drew** [dru:]	zeichnen
	picture ['pɪktʃə]	Bild
	job [dʒɒb]	Aufgabe; Tätigkeit

Station 1

Irregular verbs in Station 1

to **do** [du:]	**did** [dɪd]	**done** [dʌn]	machen; tun
to **see** [si:]	**saw** [sɔ:]	**seen** [si:n]	sehen
to **buy** [baɪ]	**bought** [bɔ:t]	**bought** [bɔ:t]	kaufen
to **feed** [fi:d]	**fed** [fed]	**fed** [fed]	füttern
to **go** [gəʊ]	**went** [went]	**gone** [gɒn]	gehen; fahren
to **hear** [hɪə]	**heard** [hɜ:d]	**heard** [hɜ:d]	hören

to **take** [teɪk]	**took** [tʊk]	**taken** [ˈteɪkn]	nehmen; mitnehmen; bringen; mitbringen
to **send** [send]	**sent** [sent]	**sent** [sent]	schicken; senden
to **have** [hæv]	**had** [hæd]	**had** [hæd]	haben; essen
to **lay** [leɪ]	**laid** [leɪd]	**laid** [leɪd]	decken; legen
to **make** [meɪk]	**made** [meɪd]	**made** [meɪd]	machen
to **eat** [iːt]	**ate** [eɪt]	**eaten** [ˈiːtn]	essen
to **sweep** [swiːp]	**swept** [swept]	**swept** [swept]	fegen

Jobs around the house

to **do the shopping** [ˌduː ðə ˈʃɒpɪŋ]	Einkäufe machen; Besorgungen machen
to **take the rubbish out** [ˌteɪk ðə ˈrʌbɪʃ‿aʊt]	den Müll rausbringen
to **tidy (up) your bedroom** [ˌtaɪdi ʌp jɔː ˈbedrʊm]	dein Schlafzimmer aufräumen
to **clean your football boots** [ˌkliːn jɔː ˈfʊtbɔːl buːts]	deine Fußballschuhe putzen
to **sweep the floor** [ˌswiːp ðə ˈflɔː]	den Fußboden fegen
to **lay the table** [ˌleɪ ðə ˈteɪbl]	den Tisch decken
to **do the washing up** [ˌduː ðə ˈwɒʃɪŋ‿ʌp]	abspülen

to take bottles to the bottle bank ['teɪk ˌbɒtlz tə ðə 'bɒtl bæŋk]	die Flaschen zum Altglascontainer bringen
to clear the table [ˌklɪə ðə 'teɪbl]	den Tisch abräumen
to hoover my bedroom [ˌhu:və maɪ 'bedrʊm]	mein Schlafzimmer staubsaugen

p. 30	**actor** ['æktə]	Schauspieler; Schauspielerin
	job [dʒɒb]	Arbeit; Beruf
	just [dʒʌst]	gerade (eben); soeben
	to **arrive** [ə'raɪv]	ankommen
	flight [flaɪt]	Flug
	already [ɔ:l'redi]	schon; bereits
	to **finish** ['fɪnɪʃ]	fertigstellen; vervollständigen
	list [lɪst]	Liste
	to **wait** [weɪt]	warten
	not ... yet [nɒt ... 'jet]	noch nicht
	supermarket ['su:pəˌmɑ:kɪt]	Supermarkt
	2moro (tomorrow) [tə'mɒrəʊ]	morgen
	to **learn** [lɜ:n]	lernen
	lines [laɪnz]	*hier:* Text
	interview ['ɪntəvju:]	Interview; Befragung
	It's a date. [ˌɪts‿ə 'deɪt]	Abgemacht!
	gr8 (great) [greɪt]	großartig; toll
	CU (See you!) ['si: ˌju]	Bis später!
	bus stop ['bʌs ˌstɒp]	Bushaltestelle
p. 31	**You're a star.** [ˌjɔ:r‿ə 'stɑ:]	Du bist fantastisch.
	boot [bu:t]	Stiefel
p. 32	to **text** [tekst]	eine SMS schreiben
	website ['websaɪt]	Website
p. 33	**vocabulary** [və'kæbjəlri]	Vokabular; Wortschatz

Station 2

Irregular verbs in Station 2

to forget [fə'get]	**forgot** [fə'gɒt]	**forgotten** [fə'gɒtn]	vergessen
to **win** [wɪn]	**won** [wʌn]	**won** [wʌn]	gewinnen; siegen
to **be** [bi:]	**was** [wɒz] / **were** [wɜ:]	**been** [bi:n]	sein
to **make** [meɪk]	**made** [meɪd]	**made** [meɪd]	machen; tun; bilden
to **take** [teɪk]	**took** [tʊk]	**taken** ['teɪkn]	hinbringen
to **break** [breɪk]	**broke** [brəʊk]	**broken** ['brəʊkn]	brechen; kaputt machen
to **wear** [weə]	**wore** [wɔ:]	**worn** [wɔ:n]	tragen

Jobs

director [dɪ'rektə]	Regisseur; Regisseurin
hairdresser ['heəˌdresə]	Friseur; Friseurin
engineer [ˌendʒɪ'nɪə]	Ingenieur; Ingenieurin; Techniker; Technikerin
waiter ['weɪtə]	Kellner
doctor ['dɒktə]	Arzt; Ärztin
nurse [nɜ:s]	Krankenschwester; Krankenpfleger
lorry driver ['lɒri ˌdraɪvə]	LKW-Fahrer; LKW-Fahrerin
builder ['bɪldə]	Bauarbeiter; Bauarbeiterin

	shop assistant ['ʃɒp‿əˌsɪstnt]	Verkäufer; Verkäuferin
	chef [ʃef]	Koch; Köchin
	vet [vet]	Tierarzt; Tierärztin
p. 34	**how many** [ˌhaʊ 'meni]	wie viele
	to **act** [ækt]	spielen
	ever ['evə]	jemals
	nervous ['nɜːvəs]	nervös; aufgeregt
	embarrassed [ɪm'bærəst]	verlegen
	young [jʌŋ]	jung
	Have you ever been to ...? [hæv ju 'evə ˌbiːn tə]	Warst du schon in ...?
	Have you finished yet? [ˌhæv juː 'fɪnɪʃt jet]	Seid ihr schon fertig?
	yet [jet]	schon
p. 36	**which** [wɪtʃ]	welche
	grandma ['grænmaː]	Oma
p. 37	**Italy** ['ɪtəli]	Italien
	Spain [speɪn]	Spanien
	Turkey ['tɜːki]	Türkei
	would [wʊd]	würde(n)
	what [wɒt]	welche
	amazing [ə'meɪzɪŋ]	unglaublich; toll; erstaunlich
	another [ə'nʌðə]	ein andere; noch ein
	would like [wʊd 'laɪk]	würde(n) gern; hätte(n) gern

Reading corner

p. 38	**pantomime** ['pæntəmaɪm]	Weihnachtstheaterstück
	audition [ɔː'dɪʃn]	Vorspielen; Vorsprechen; Vorsingen; Vortanzen
	... looking at an advert. [ˌlʊkɪŋ ət‿ən 'ædvɜːt]	... schaut sich eine Anzeige an.
	child *(sg)* [tʃaɪld], **children** *(pl)* [tʃɪldrn]	Kind

	a.m. [ˌeɪ'em]	vormittags *(Uhrzeit)*
	p.m. [ˌpi:'em]	nachmittags *(Uhrzeit)*
	theatre ['θɪətə]	Theater
	registration [ˌrədʒɪ'streɪʃn]	Anmeldung
	chance [tʃɑ:ns]	Chance; Gelegenheit
	if [ɪf]	wenn; falls
	to **miss** [mɪs]	verpassen
	minute ['mɪnɪt]	Minute
	to **be stuck** [bi 'stʌk]	feststecken
	behind [bɪ'haɪnd]	hinter
	sofa ['səʊfə]	Sofa
	to **hurry** ['hʌri]	sich beeilen
p. 39	**past** [pɑ:st]	nach *(bei Uhrzeitangaben)*
	lady ['leɪdi]	Dame; Frau
	too [tu:]	zu
	It's my fault. [ɪts ˌmaɪ 'fɔ:lt]	Es ist meine Schuld.
	to **go on** [ˌgəʊ‿'ɒn]	*hier:* hineingehen
	judge [dʒʌdʒ]	Juror; Jurorin
	corridor ['kɒrɪdɔ:]	Gang; Flur
	in [ɪn]	drinnen

Film corner

p. 41	**ticket** ['tɪkɪt]	*hier:* Karte
	acting workshop ['æktɪŋ ˌwɜ:kʃɒp]	Schauspielworkshop
	to **remember** [rɪ'membə]	sich merken; sich erinnern (an)
	just [dʒʌst]	nur
	to **believe** [bɪ'li:v]	glauben
	yourself [jɔ:'self]	dich selbst
	to **panic** ['pænɪk]	panisch werden
	who [hu:]	*hier:* die; welche
	in the world [ɪn ðə 'wɜ:ld]	auf der Welt

Speaking skills

p. 46	**ill** [ɪl]	krank; schlecht
	sore throat [ˌsɔː 'θrəʊt]	Halsschmerzen
	headache ['hedeɪk]	Kopfschmerzen; Kopfweh
	to **have a look** [ˌhæv‿ə 'lʊk]	anschauen
	to **hurt** [hɜːt], **hurt** [hɜːt], **hurt** [hɜːt]	weh tun; verletzen
	a little [ə 'lɪtl]	ein bisschen
	to **drink** [drɪŋk], **drank** [dræŋk], **drunk** [drʌŋk]	trinken
	leg [leg]	Bein
	stomach ache ['stʌmək ˌeɪk]	Bauchweh; Bauchschmerzen
	broken ['brəʊkn]	past participle von *to break* (brechen; zerbrechen)
p. 47	**mouth** [maʊθ]	Mund
	stomach ['stʌmək]	Magen; Bauch
	head [hed]	Kopf
	ear [ɪə]	Ohr
	patient ['peɪʃnt]	Patient; Patientin
	tablet ['tæblət]	Tablette
	a lot [ə 'lɒt]	sehr

Du kannst die unregelmäßigen Verben mit einem Spiel zu zweit (oder zu mehreren) leichter lernen: Schreibe alle Verbformen jeweils auf einen Zettel und stecke sie in eine Schachtel. Ziehe einen Zettel und sage die Grundform. Sage dann die beiden anderen Verbformen dazu. Dein Partner oder deine Partnerin sagt, wie das Verb auf Deutsch heißt.

A: Drink – drank, drunk.

B: Trinken.

1 Complete the text.

crowd | job | jumble | organized
player | star | stage

My football club wants to go on a trip to Germany.

We needed money so we ______________ a ______________ sale. Lots of people came because a famous football ______________ was there. He stood on the __________ and spoke to the __________ . He said football was a great sport and he loved his __________ . Everyone cheered and I have a selfie with the __________ . It was great! We can now go to Germany next summer.

2 Complete the table.

Infinitive	Simple past	Pres. perfect (has/have ...)	German (Infinitive)
1. ________	________	________	kaufen
2. do	________	________	________
3. ________	went	________	________
4. ________	________	heard	________
5. ________	________	________	sehen
6. take	________	________	________

3 Look at the pictures. What has he done?

texted | taken | cleaned | done | tidied

1.  He has ______________________________ ______________________________.

2.  She has ______________________________ ______________________________.

3.  He has ______________________________ ______________________________.

4.  She has ______________________________ ______________________________.

5. 

He has ______________________________ ______________________________.

4 Write the right word.

just | already | (not) yet

1. Let's go to see the Hobbit. – No, I've ______________ seen it.
2. Have you done your homework? – Yes, I've ______________ finished it now.
3. Have you tidied your room? – No, I haven't done it _______ .

5 Write the text message in words.

6 Find eight words and write them down.

A	L	C	B	O	O	T	L	R	C	F
N	I	N	T	E	R	V	I	E	W	L
X	N	F	O	Q	N	N	S	E	B	I
W	E	B	S	I	T	E	T	Z	U	G
J	S	E	D	A	C	T	O	R	L	H
S	U	P	E	R	M	A	R	K	E	T

1. ______________ 5. ______________

2. ______________ 6. ______________

3. ______________ 7. ______________

4. ______________ 8. ______________

7 Write their jobs.

1.  ______________________________

2.  ______________________________

3.  ______________________________

4.  ______________________________

5.  ______________________________

6. 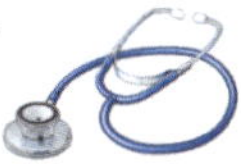 ______________________________

7.  ______________________________

8 Put in the right form of the verb.

1. Where's your ticket? – Oh, I'm sorry. I've ______________ (forget) it.
2. You're late. Where have you __________ (be)?
3. And the score is 2 – 1. United have __________ (win) again!
4. Aren't you hungry? I've just __________ (make) the dinner.

9 Find the words.

▼ 1. I fell on stage and I felt … .
4. I felt … before I sang my song on stage.
6. Have you done question 8 …?

▶ 2. His new song was … – I was surprised it was so good.
3. Barcelona and Madrid are in this country.
5. I'm sorry. I've … my homework. I don't usually forget it.
7. Have you … been to Turkey?
8. My grandfather isn't … . He's old.

10 Write the times with a.m. and p.m.

1. 14:00 ____________________
2. 8:00 ____________________
3. 11:59 ____________________
4. 22:15 ____________________

11 What can you see?

1.  one ______________________

2.  many ______________________

3. 

____

4.  ______________________

12 Write the words in English.

1. sich erinnern — I ______________ you!
2. panisch werden — Don't ______________ ! You're OK.
3. glauben — Do you ______________ in aliens?
4. üben — I ______________ the saxophone every day.
5. sich beeilen — We're late. We must ______________ .

13 Write the words.

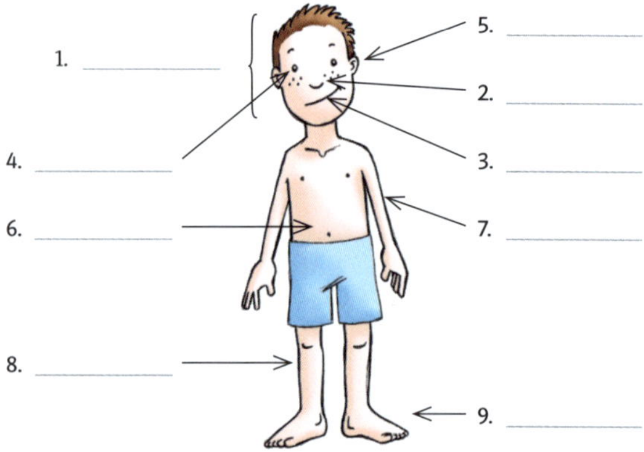

14 Complete the dialogue.

Doctor: Hello Jay. How are you today?

Jay: Oh, I have a stomach ________ and a ________ throat.

Doctor: Does your throat ________ when you drink?

Jay: Yes, and I have a ________________ .

Doctor: Does your head hurt when you move it?

Jay: Yes, and it hurts when I think. Can you give me some ______________ ?

Doctor: No, Jay. Go home and go to bed and no TV.

Jay: But doctor, I'm not so ________ !

●15 Ready for the party?

a) Find the words.

shigwan pu | ti | oorfl | ecak | telba
lettob nabk | gopnishp | blestot | bushbir

b) Put in the right verb forms and write in the words from a).

Luke has ________ (do) the ___________ and he has ________ (take) the ___________ out! Irina and Jamie have ___________ (make) a ________ . Dad has ________ (sweep) the ________ .

Mum has already ________ (do) the ______________ and has ________ (take) the ________ to the ______________ . Jamie has ________ (lay) the ________ and wants to put the cake on it. But … Oh no! Sherlock has ____________ (eat) ________ .

●16 What are their jobs?

1. Anna isn't a doctor but works in a hospital. ______________________
2. Andy drives a lorry. ______________________
3. Tanya builds houses and flats. ______________________
4. Tom helps people in a shop. ______________________
5. Linda works in a kitchen. ______________________
6. Is your cat ill? Murad can help. ______________________

Unit 3 London life

Way in

p. 48	**archive** ['ɑ:kaɪv]	Archiv
	blog [blɒg]	Blog; Internettagebuch
	everyone ['evriwʌn]	alle
	back home [bæk 'həʊm]	zu Hause
	Poland ['pəʊlənd]	Polen
	boat trip ['bəʊt ˌtrɪp]	Bootsfahrt; Schiffsfahrt
	sight [saɪt]	Sehenswürdigkeit
	building ['bɪldɪŋ]	Gebäude
	big wheel [ˌbɪg 'wi:l]	Riesenrad
	to **build** [bɪld], **built** [bɪlt], **built** [bɪlt]	bauen
	worker ['wɜ:kə]	Arbeiter; Arbeiterin
	UK [ˌju:'keɪ]	Vereinigtes Königreich von Großbritannien und Nordirland
	France [frɑ:ns]	Frankreich
	the Netherlands [ðə 'neðələndz]	die Niederlande
	the Czech Republic [ðə ˌtʃek rɪ'pʌblɪk]	Tschechien
p. 49	**the most famous** [ðə 'məʊst ˌfeɪməs]	der berühmteste
	clock tower ['klɒk ˌtaʊə]	Uhrenturm
	to **abseil** ['æbseɪl]	sich abseilen
	tower ['taʊə]	Turm
	step [step]	Stufe
	about [ə'baʊt]	ungefähr; circa; etwa
	prison ['prɪzn]	Gefängnis
	royal ['rɔɪəl]	königlich
	copy ['kɒpi]	Kopie
	It was built … [ˌɪt wəz 'bɪlt]	Es wurde … gebaut.
	writer ['raɪtə]	Schriftsteller; Schriftstellerin
	than [ðæn]	als

	ago [ə'gəʊ]	vor
p. 48	**wheel** [wi:l]	Rad
	restaurant ['restrɒnt]	Restaurant
p. 49	**really** ['rɪəli]	echt

Station 1

Sights

church [tʃɜ:tʃ]	Kirche
castle ['kɑ:sl]	Schloss; Burg
stadium ['steɪdiəm]	Stadion
market ['mɑ:kɪt]	Markt
town hall [ˌtaʊn 'hɔ:l]	Rathaus
bridge [brɪdʒ]	Brücke
square [skweə]	Platz
mosque [mɒsk]	Moschee
city centre [ˌsɪti 'sentə]	Stadtzentrum; Stadtmitte
lake [leɪk]	See
monument ['mɒnjəmənt]	Denkmal
lookout point ['lʊkaʊt ˌpɔɪnt]	Aussichtspunkt

Numbers 101 – 200,000

a / one hundred and one 101 [ə/wʌn ˌhʌndrəd‿ən 'wʌn]	hunderteins
a / one hundred and two 102 [ə/wʌn ˌhʌndrəd‿ən 'tu:]	hundertzwei
a / one hundred and ten 110 [ə/wʌn ˌhʌndrəd‿ən 'ten]	hundertzehn

two hundred 200 [tuː 'hʌndrəd]	zwei hundert
three hundred 300 [θriː 'hʌndrəd]	dreihundert
four hundred and fifty-one 451 [fɔː 'hʌndrəd‿ən ˌfɪftiwʌn]	vierhunderteinundfünfzig
a / one thousand 1,000 [ə/wʌn 'θaʊznd]	eintausend

p. 50	**up** [ʌp]	hinauf; oben
	height [haɪt]	Höhe
	fact [fækt]	Fakt; Tatsache
	to **weigh** [weɪ]	wiegen
	tonne [tʌn]	Tonne
	taxi ['tæksi]	Taxi
	bell [bel]	Glocke
	dome [dəʊm]	Kuppel
	thought [θɔːt]	simple past, past participle von *to think* (denken)
	tall [tɔːl]	groß; hoch
	as … as [əz … əz]	so … wie
	telephone box ['telɪfəʊn ˌbɒks]	Telefonzelle
	even ['iːvn]	noch; sogar
	pretty ['prɪti]	hübsch
	expensive [ɪk'spensɪv]	teuer
p. 51	**TV studio** [ˌtiː'viː ˌstjuːdiəʊ]	Fernsehstudio
	office ['ɒfɪs]	Büro
	floor [flɔː]	Stockwerk
	visitor ['vɪzɪtə]	Besucher; Besucherin
	to **sunbathe** ['sʌnbeɪð]	sonnenbaden
	low [ləʊ]	niedrig
	to **guess** [ges]	erraten; raten; überlegen
p. 52	**any** ['eni]	irgendein
	Europe ['jʊərəp]	Europa

burger ['bɜ:gə]	Hamburger
fast [fɑ:st]	schnell

Station 2

Adjectives for clothes

cheap [tʃi:p]	billig
expensive [ɪk'spensɪv]	teuer
large [lɑ:dʒ]	groß
small [smɔ:l]	klein
short [ʃɔ:t]	kurz
long [lɒŋ]	lang
tight [taɪt]	eng; fest
loose [lu:s]	locker; lose
fashionable ['fæʃnəbl]	modisch
unfashionable [ʌn'fæʃnəbl]	unmodisch
comfortable ['kʌmftəbl]	bequem; angenehm
uncomfortable [ʌn'kʌmftəbl]	unbequem; unangenehm
patterned ['pætənd]	gemustert
plain [pleɪn]	schlicht; einfach

p. 54	**department store** [dɪ'pɑ:tmənt ˌstɔ:]	Kaufhaus
	sale [seɪl]	Schlussverkauf; Ausverkauf
	top [tɒp]	Top; Oberteil
	department [dɪ'pɑ:tmənt]	Abteilung
	these [ði:z]	diese (hier)
	those [ðəʊz]	jene
	to **suit** [su:t]	stehen; passen
	size [saɪz]	Größe
	next [nekst]	als Nächstes

	to **look for** ['lʊk fə]	suchen nach
	isn't it? ['ɪznt‿ɪt]	nicht wahr?; stimmt's?
	may [meɪ]	vielleicht
	in the end [ɪn ði 'end]	schließlich; zum Schluss
	not … any [ˌnɒt … eni]	kein
	shop assistant ['ʃɒp‿əˌsɪstnt]	Verkäufer; Verkäuferin
	receipt [ri'si:t]	Quittung
p. 56	**colourful** ['kʌləfl]	bunt
	language ['læŋgwɪdʒ]	Sprache
	British ['brɪtɪʃ]	britisch

Reading corner

p. 58	**drama** ['drɑ:mə]	Theater; Drama
	play [pleɪ]	Theaterstück
	boss [bɒs]	Boss; Chef
	to **own** [əʊn]	besitzen
	part [pɑ:t]	Rolle
	landlord ['lændlɔ:d]	Eigentümer
	to **ask for** ['ɑ:sk fɔ:]	bitten um
	rent [rent]	Miete
	land [lænd]	Land
	to **pay** [peɪ], **paid** [peɪd], **paid** [peɪd]	bezahlen
	to **move (house)** [mu:v]	umziehen
	builder ['bɪldə]	Bauarbeiter; Bauarbeiterin
	to **carry** ['kæri]	tragen; befördern
	brick by brick [ˌbrɪk baɪ 'brɪk]	Stein für Stein
	plank [plæŋk]	Brett; Planke
	across [ə'krɒs]	über
	heavy ['hevi]	schwer; stark
p. 59	**by** [baɪ]	von
	important [ɪm'pɔ:tnt]	wichtig; einflussreich
	as [æz]	als
	cannon ['kænən]	Kanone
	cannon ball ['kænən ˌbɔ:l]	Kanonenkugel
	to **hit** [hɪt], **hit** [hɪt], **hit** [hɪt]	treffen; schlagen

	roof [ru:f]	Dach
	to **be on fire** [ˌbi: ɒn ˈfaɪə]	brennen
	luckily [ˈlʌkɪli]	glücklicherweise
	hurt [hɜ:t]	verletzt
	help [help]	Hilfe
	fire engine [ˈfaɪər‿ˌendʒɪn]	Feuerwehrauto
	to **burn down** [bɜ:n ˈdaʊn], **burnt down** [bɜ:nt ˈdaʊn], **burnt down** [bɜ:nt ˈdaʊn]	niederbrennen; verbrennen
	carpenter [ˈkɑ:pəntə]	Zimmermann; Zimmerin; Tischler; Tischlerin
	right [raɪt]	*hier:* also
	tool [tu:l]	Werkzeug; Gerät

Film corner

p. 61	**sunglasses** *(pl)* [ˈsʌnˌglɑ:sɪz]	Sonnenbrille
	to **wait for** [ˈweɪt fɔ:]	warten auf
	to **go sightseeing** [gəʊ ˈsaɪtsi:ɪŋ]	eine Besichtigungstour machen
	sticker [ˈstɪkə]	Aufkleber
	stallholder [ˈstɔ:lˌhəʊldə]	Standinhaber; Standinhaberin
	each [i:tʃ]	pro Stück
	How about ...? [ˌhaʊ‿əˈbaʊt]	Wie wäre es mit ...?
	a pair of [ə ˈpeər‿əv]	ein Paar
	price [praɪs]	Preis
	real [rɪəl]	echt; richtig; wirklich
	bargain [ˈbɑ:gɪn]	Schnäppchen
	to **sound** [saʊnd]	klingen

Listening skills

Airport words

departure [dɪ'pɑːtʃə]	Abflug
gate [geɪt]	Gate; Ausgang
last call [ˌlɑːst 'kɔːl]	letzter Aufruf
boarding ['bɔːdɪŋ]	an Bord gehen
cancelled ['kænslt]	annulliert
delayed [dɪ'leɪd]	verspätet
check-in ['tʃekɪn]	Gepäckaufgabe
toilet ['tɔɪlət]	Toilette

p. 66	**airport** ['eəpɔːt]	Flughafen
p. 67	**announcement** [ə'naʊnsmənt]	Durchsage; Ankündigung
	passenger ['pæsndʒə]	Passagier; Passagierin
	plane [pleɪn]	Flugzeug
	to **fly** [flaɪ], **flew** [fluː], **flown** [fləʊn]	fliegen
	information desk [ɪnfə'meɪʃn ˌdesk]	Information

Sammle Wörter, die Ähnlichkeiten oder Unterschiede haben, z.B. Wörter mit zwei Bedeutungen:

tragen ↗ to carry ↘ to wear

Preis ↗ prize (Gewinn) ↘ price (Kosten)

oder gleich klingende Wörter:

to s**ee** – sehen | s**ea** – Meer

w**i**tch – Hexe | wh**i**ch – welche

to m**ee**t – treffen | m**ea**t – Fleisch

hour – Stunde | our – unser

1 Complete the text.

ago | big wheel | boat trip | clock tower | city | royal | buildings | restaurant | sights | prison | built

Last weekend we went on a day trip to London. One day isn't much time to see the ________ so we started with a ____________ on the Thames. You can see a lot of the most famous ____________ from the river and the tour guide told us all about them. It was great.

Then we went on the London Eye. That's the ______________ on the Thames. It was ________ from 1998 to 2000. The weather was great so we saw most of the famous ___________ and parks in London from there. We also saw Big Ben – that's the famous __________________ .

Then we visited the Tower of London. It was a ________ home and a long time ________ there was a __________ there.

In the evening we went to a _______________ and ate Indian food. It was great, and next time we want to stay for longer.

2 Write the countries in English.

1. Vereinigtes Königreich ______________________
2. Frankreich ______________________
3. die Niederlande ______________________
4. Tschechien ______________________
5. Spanien ______________________
6. Australien ______________________
7. Türkei ______________________

3 Write the words in English and German.

1.  ______________ ______________
2.  ______________ ______________
3.  ______________ ______________
4.  ______________ ______________
5. 

______________ ______________
6.  ______________ ______________
7.  ______________ ______________

4 Write the numbers.

1. 101 ______________________________
2. 582 ______________________________
3. 334 ______________________________
4. 3021 ______________________________
5. 9219 ______________________________

5 What do you remember? Write the words.

1

________ : 135 metres

It ________ 2,100 ________ .

2

The tower is 96 metres ________ . The ________ weighs 300 kg.

1. ______________________________
2. ______________________________
3. ______________________________

3

It was ________ in 1720.

The ________ has 530 steps.

6 What is it?

1. It's in a building. People work in it. ______________
2. They make TV programmes here. ______________
3. Another word for a tourist. ______________
4. Do this on the beach to get browner. ______________
5. Another word for beautiful. ______________
6. It's information and it's true. ______________

7 Find the words and complete the dialogue.

isntittopsuitssizetheseshopassistantlookfor

Jane: What do you think of this ______________ ?

Ellen: That colour really ______________ you, but it's too small, ______________ ?

Jane: Yes, can you ______________ the next ______________ , please?

Ellen: OK … Sorry, I can't see any in size 10.

Jane: Can you ask a ______________ , please?

Ellen: Yes, of course … Here, what about ______________ jeans?

Jane: Oh, they're great. Thanks!

8 Find six pairs. Write them in English and German.

T	E	X	P	E	N	S	I	V	E
C	J	L	A	N	T	H	I	G	H
H	S	L	L	O	Y	O	U	N	G
E	C	O	L	O	U	R	F	U	L
A	A	W	V	L	U	T	U	P	O
P	T	E	R	R	I	B	L	E	N
F	A	N	T	A	S	T	I	C	G
O	X	O	L	D	R	Y	V	K	I
W	E	T	E	Z	G	R	E	Y	B

1. dry – wet ______ *trocken – nass* ______
2. ______ ______
3. ______ ______
4. ______ ______
5. ______ ______
6. ______ ______
7. ______ ______

9 Find the words.

▼ 1. This is a person in a car or on a plane.
2. It's sunny so you wear these.
4. Hey! That isn't a … banana. Don't eat it.
5. It's too expensive. The … is too high.

▶ 3. Planes leave from an … .
6. I'm going to … to Australia (by plane).
7. Wow, that's cheap. It's a real … .
8. How much are the T-shirts? – Twelve pounds … .
9. I want to put … on my school bag so it looks better.

10 Write the English words.

1. Moschee ______________
2. See ______________
3. Denkmal ______________
4. Platz ______________
5. Stockwerk ______________

lofor | rasque | kael | quemso | ontenumm

11 Write the opposites.

1. tight ______________
2. fashionable ______________
3. patterned ______________
4. comfortable ______________

12 Write the missing words.

Last year we came home one night and saw our house ______________ fire. The ______________ engines came – but they were too late. Our house ______________ ______________ . ______________ no one was hurt. We still owned the land so we built the house again brick by ______________ .

●13 What can you see in the pictures?

1.  ______________________
2.  ______________________
3.  ______________________
4.  ______________________
5.  ______________________
6.  ______________________
7.  ______________________

●14 Write the missing words.

1. My mum's __________ is nice. They work well together.
2. My grandma lives __________ the street from us.
3. My brother has a __________ in the play – he's an alien.
4. My mum works __________ a carpenter.
5. His new play is a __________ , but it's funny too.
6. I want to be an actor __________ I leave school.

Unit 4 Food and drink

Way in

Food

rice [raɪs]	Reis
coconut ['kəʊkənʌt]	Kokosnuss
kidney bean ['kɪdni ˌbiːn]	Kidneybohne
vegetable (veg) ['vedʒtəbl]	Gemüse
pasta ['pæstə]	Pasta; Nudeln
salad ['sæləd]	Salat
pierogi [pjɜ'rɔgi]	Pirogge
dumpling ['dʌmplɪŋ]	Kloß
cabbage ['kæbɪdʒ]	Kohl; Kraut
sausage ['sɒsɪdʒ]	Wurst; Bratwurst
onion ['ʌnjən]	Zwiebel
pasty ['pæsti]	Pastete
pie [paɪ]	Kuchen; Pastete
potato *(sg)* [pə'teɪtəʊ], **potatoes** *(pl)* [pə'teɪtəʊz]	Kartoffel
carrot ['kærət]	Karotte
chicken ['tʃɪkɪn]	Hühnchen
curry ['kʌri]	Curry
spice [spaɪs]	Gewürz
yogurt ['jɒgət]	Joghurt
bread [bred]	Brot
pork [pɔːk]	Schweinefleisch
potato salad [pəˌteɪtəʊ 'sæləd]	Kartoffelsalat

p. 68	**drink** [drɪŋk]	Getränk
p. 69	**Jamaican** [dʒə'meɪkən]	jamaikanisch
	yummy ['jʌmi]	lecker
	sort [sɔ:t]	Sorte; Art
	delicious [dɪ'lɪʃəs]	köstlich
	It's made with … [ˌɪts 'meɪd wɪð]	Es wird aus … gemacht.

Station 1

Irregular verbs in Station 1

to choose [tʃu:z]	chose [tʃəʊz]	chosen ['tʃəʊzn]	auswählen; wählen
to spend [spend]	spent [spent]	spent [spent]	ausgeben; verbringen

Meals at school

packed lunch [ˌpækt 'lʌnʃ]	Lunchpaket; Vesper
mashed potatoes [ˌmæʃt pə'teɪtəʊz]	Kartoffelbrei
apple crumble [ˌæpl 'krʌmbl]	Apfelauflauf *(mit Streuseln bedeckt)*
custard ['kʌstəd]	Vanillesauce
ham [hæm]	Schinken
pasta bake [ˌpæstə 'beɪk]	Nudelauflauf
pudding ['pʊdɪŋ]	Nachspeise; Pudding
beef [bi:f]	Rindfleisch
chilli ['tʃɪli]	Chili
garlic ['gɑ:lɪk]	Knoblauch

tomato *(sg)* [tə'mɑ:təʊ], **tomatoes** *(pl)* [tə'mɑ:təʊz]	Tomate
soup [su:p]	Suppe
strawberry ['strɔ:bri]	Erdbeere
spaghetti [spə'geti]	Spaghetti
sauce [sɔ:s]	Soße
lemon ['lemən]	Zitrone
cheesecake ['tʃi:skeɪk]	Käsekuchen
lasagne [lə'zænjə]	Lasagne
spring roll [ˌsprɪŋ 'rəʊl]	Frühlingsrolle
pancake ['pænkeɪk]	Pfannkuchen
jacket potato [ˌdʒækɪt pə'teɪtəʊ]	Ofenkartoffel
lamb [læm]	Lamm
moussaka [mu'sɑ:kə]	Moussaka

p. 70	**meal** [mi:l]	Mahlzeit; Essen
	internet ['ɪntənet]	Internet
	news [nju:z]	Neuigkeit(en); Nachricht(en)
	survey ['sɜ:veɪ]	Umfrage
	main course [ˌmeɪn 'kɔ:s]	Hauptgericht
	dessert [dɪ'zɜ:t]	Nachspeise
	usually ['ju:ʒli]	normalerweise; gewöhnlich
	allergy ['ælədʒi]	Allergie
	allergic to [ə'lɜ:dʒɪk tə]	allergisch gegen
	fingerprint ['fɪŋgəprɪnt]	Fingerabdruck
	payment machine ['peɪmənt ˌməʃi:n]	Bezahlautomat
	machine [mə'ʃi:n]	Automat; Maschine
	to **work** [wɜ:k]	*hier:* funktionieren
	quick [kwɪk]	schnell
	many ['meni]	viele
	answer ['ɑ:nsə]	Antwort

	result [rɪ'zʌlt]	Ergebnis
	fried [fraɪd]	(in der Pfanne) gebraten
p. 71	**starter** ['stɑ:tə]	Vorspeise
p. 72	**cash** [kæʃ]	(mit) Bargeld
p. 73	**dog biscuit** ['dɒg ˌbɪskɪt]	Hundekeks
	person ['pɜ:sn]	Person; Mensch

Station 2

Things for meals

knife *(sg)* [naɪf], **knives** *(pl)* [naɪvz]	Messer
fork [fɔ:k]	Gabel
spoon [spu:n]	Löffel
salt [sɔ:lt]	Salz
ketchup ['ketʃʌp]	Ketchup
plate [pleɪt]	Teller
glass [glɑ:s]	Glas
pepper ['pepə]	Pfeffer
cup [kʌp]	Tasse
napkin ['næpkɪn]	Serviette
bowl [bəʊl]	Schale; Schälchen; Schüssel
mayonnaise [ˌmeɪə'neɪz]	Mayonnaise
teaspoon ['ti:spu:n]	Teelöffel
straw [strɔ:]	Trinkhalm
mustard ['mʌstəd]	Senf
tray [treɪ]	Tablett
toothpick ['tu:θpɪk]	Zahnstocher

p. 74	**food stall** ['fu:d ˌstɔ:l]	Essensstand
	menu ['menju:]	Speisekarte
	jerk [dʒɜ:k]	*in Gewürzen mariniertes und über Holzfeuer gegrilltes Essen*
	wrap [ræp]	Wrap *(Tortillafladen zum Einwickeln)*
	free range [ˌfri: 'reɪndʒ]	Freiland-
	veggie bean cake [ˌvedʒi 'bi:n keɪk]	*vegetarisches Bohnengericht*
	mama ['mæmə]	Mama
	fresh [freʃ]	frisch
	combination [ˌkɒmbɪ'neɪʃn]	Kombination
	plantain ['plænteɪn]	Kochbanane
	will [wɪl]	werden
	spicy ['spaɪsi]	würzig; pikant
	to **try** [traɪ]	probieren; versuchen
	juice [dʒu:s]	Saft
	thirsty ['θɜ:sti]	durstig
	to **order** ['ɔ:də]	bestellen
	anything to drink ['eniθɪŋ tə 'drɪŋk]	etwas zu trinken
	anything ['eniθɪŋ]	irgendetwas
	I've (I have) got [ˌaɪv 'gɒt]	ich habe
	note [nəʊt]	*hier:* Geldschein
	to **pay back** [ˌpeɪ 'bæk]	zurückzahlen
	won't (= will not) [wəʊnt]	nicht werden
	change [tʃeɪndʒ]	Münzgeld; Wechselgeld
	It won't be long. [ɪt ˌwəʊnt bi 'lɒŋ]	Es wird nicht lange dauern.
	over there [ˌəʊvə 'ðeə]	da drüben; dort drüben
p. 75	**tuna** ['tju:nə]	Thunfisch
	extra ['ekstrə]	zusätzlich; Zusatz-
p. 76	**any** ['eni]	irgendwelche
p. 77	to **watch** [wɒtʃ]	*hier:* aufpassen auf
	leave [li:v], **left** [left], **left** [left]	lassen; verlassen; abfahren

Reading corner

p. 78	to **cook** [kʊk]	kochen
	TV show [ˌtiː ˈviː ˌʃəʊ]	Fernsehsendung
	teen [tiːn]	Jugend-; Teenager; Jugendliche; Jugendlicher
	chef [ʃef]	Koch; Köchin
	kid [kɪd]	Kind
	to **take part (in)** [ˌteɪk ˈpɑːt]	teilnehmen (an)
	competition [ˌkɒmpəˈtɪʃn]	Wettbewerb
	entry form [ˈentri ˌfɔːm]	Anmeldeformular
	scrambled egg [ˌskræmbld‿ˈeg]	Rührei
	to **watch** [wɒtʃ]	zuschauen
	she was making [ˌʃiː wəz ˈmeɪkɪŋ]	sie machte
	flour [flaʊə]	Mehl
	to **become** [bɪˈkʌm], **became** [bɪˈkeɪm], **become** [bɪˈkʌm]	werden
	magic [ˈmædʒɪk]	Magie; Zauberei
	magic [ˈmædʒɪk]	magisch; Zauber-
	cooking [ˈkʊkɪŋ]	Kochen
	ambition [æmˈbɪʃn]	Ziel
	own [əʊn]	eigene
	Italian [ɪˈtæliən]	italienisch; Italiener; Italienerin; Italienisch
	catering college [ˈkeɪtərɪŋ ˌkɒlɪdʒ]	Hotelfachschule
	most [məʊst]	am meisten
	teamwork [ˈtiːmwɜːk]	Teamwork
	by yourself [baɪ ˈjɔːself]	allein
	especially [ɪˈspeʃli]	besonders; vor allem
	I prefer working [aɪ prɪˈfɜː ˌwɜːkɪŋ]	ich arbeite lieber
	oven [ˈʌvn]	Backofen
	to **run about** [ˈrʌn‿əˌbaʊt]	herumrennen
	advice [ədˈvaɪs]	Rat; Ratschlag
	hard [hɑːd]	hart
	head chef [ˈhed ʃef]	Chefkoch

p. 79	**recipe** ['resɪpi]	Rezept
	of mine [əv 'maɪn]	von mir
	ingredient [ɪn'gri:diənt]	Zutat
	teaspoon *(tsp)* ['ti:spu:n]	Teelöffel *(TL)*
	piece [pi:s]	Stück
	pinch [pɪntʃ]	*hier:* Prise
	secret ['si:krət]	geheim
	method ['meθəd]	Methode
	to **add** [æd]	hinzufügen
	to **stir** [stɜ:]	rühren; umrühren
	microwave ['maɪkrəweɪv]	Mikrowelle
	second ['seknd]	Sekunde
	blue cheese [ˌblu: 'tʃi:s]	Schimmelkäse
	super ['su:pə]	super
	to **cut** [kʌt], **cut** [kʌt], **cut** [kʌt]	(sich) schneiden
	once more ['wʌns ˌmɔ:]	noch einmal
	toast [təʊst]	Toast
	proud (of) ['praʊd‿əv]	stolz (auf)
	all [ɔ:l]	ganz
	talk [tɔ:k]	Gerede
	Congratulations! [ˌkɔŋgrætjʊ'leɪʃnz]	Glückwunsch!
	tip [tɪp]	Tipp; Ratschlag

Film corner

p. 81	to **twist** [twɪst]	verdrehen; verzerren
	ankle ['æŋkl]	Fußgelenk; Fußknöchel
	basketball ['bɑ:skɪtbɔ:l]	Basketball
	to **pass** [pɑ:s]	reichen
	lemonade [ˌlemə'neɪd]	Limonade
	Help yourselves! [ˌhelp jɔ:'selvz]	Bedient euch!; Bedienen Sie sich!
	lovely ['lʌvli]	schön; herrlich; hübsch
	may [meɪ]	können; dürfen
	sausage roll [ˌsɒsɪdʒ 'rəʊl]	*Blätterteig mit Wurstfüllung*

Reading skills

p. 86	**Indian** ['ɪndiən]	indisch
	message ['mesɪdʒ]	Nachricht; Botschaft; SMS
	flyer ['flaɪə]	Flyer; Faltblatt
	dish [dɪʃ]	Gericht; Speise
	takeaway ['teɪkəweɪ]	Essen zum Mitnehmen
p. 87	**to** [tʊ]	*hier:* bis

Fertige für jede Präposition (after, about, to etc.) eine Karteikarte an und schreibe passende Wortverbindungen dazu:

about
- out and about
- to run about

after
- to look after
- after that

to
- allergic to
- from Tuesday to Sunday

1 Write the food words.

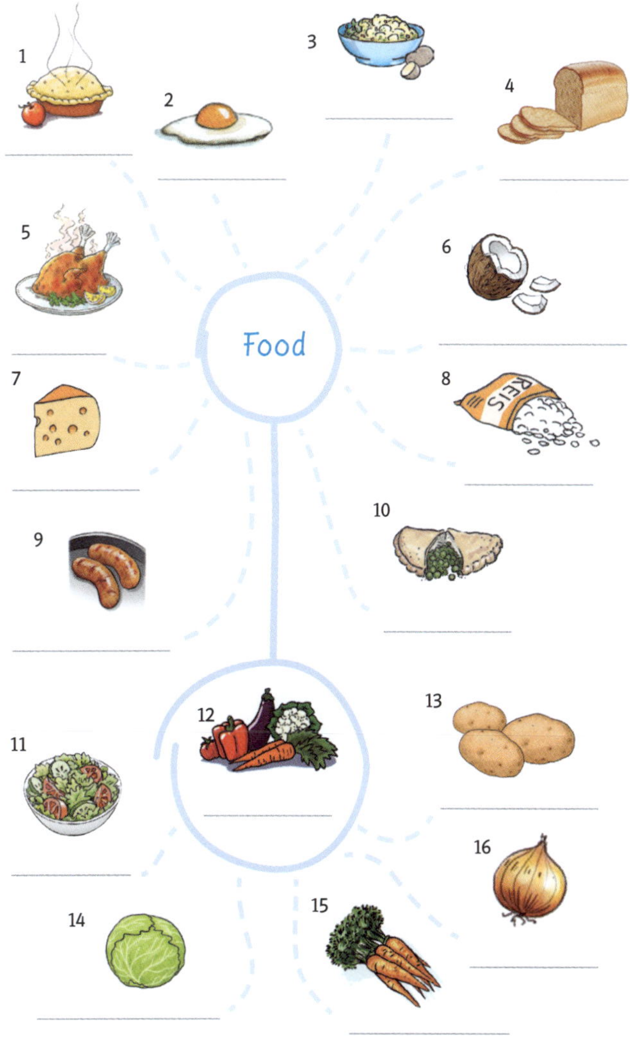

2 Write the missing words.

deliciousgrandmaJamaicanmadesortspicesyummy

My ____________ makes my favourite food. She's

____________ and she always uses lots of ____________ .

She makes a ________ of curry which is ____________ .

It's ____________ with fish, vegetables and coconut.

________ !

3 Complete the table.

Infinitive	Simple past	Pres. perfect (has/have ...)	German (Infinitive)
1. ______	______	______	auswählen
2. spend	______	______	______
3. ______	flew	______	______
4. ______	______	sounded	______

4 Find the words and write them in the right order.

anim oscure 1. ____________________

redsset 2. ____________________

rearstt 3. ____________________

5 Match the words.

1. packed — crumble
2. mashed — lunch
3. apple — bake
4. pasta — potatoes

6 Write the words.

Dave Preston often eats a school dinner in the cafeteria and he u__________ spends £3.00. He loves sausages and m__________ p__________ for his main course. He can't eat nuts because he is a__________ to them. He likes the p__________ machine because it's q__________ .

7 Complete the sentences with the English words.

1. Nachrichten — Did you hear the __________ yesterday?
2. viele — We don't have __________ tomatoes.
3. Essen — What's your favourite __________ ?
4. gebraten — I love __________ bananas.

8 Find the words.

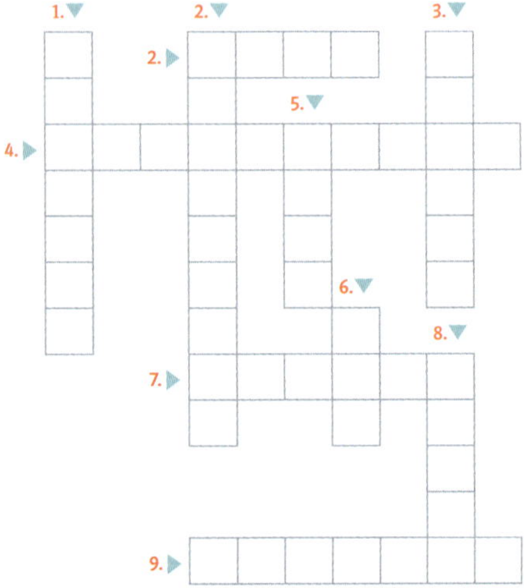

▶ 2. Eat this as a starter.
4. a small red fruit
7. It's red and you eat it in salads.
9. another word for dessert

▼ 1. Eat this warm or cold on desserts.
2. They eat this a lot in Italy.
3. a vegetable; like an onion
5. meat from a cow
6. another meat
8. like garlic; hurts your eyes

9 What are the words?

1. ______________________ 4. ______________________

2. ______________________ 5. ______________________

3. ______________________ 6. ______________________

10 Find the wrong word and write it in German.

1. cash • change • extra • note — *zusätzlich/Zusatz-*
2. plantain • ketchup • pepper • salt ______________________
3. apple • banana • plantain • wrap ______________________
4. free range • fresh • napkin • spicy ______________________
5. combination • fork • knife • spoon ______________________
6. fried • menu • spicy • yummy ______________________
7. juice • tea • thirsty • water ______________________
8. beef • ham • order • tuna ______________________

11 Find 11 words. Write them next to the German.

V	C	I	T	E	E	N	L	A	S
F	T	E	A	S	P	O	O	N	I
L	C	R	E	C	I	P	E	K	O
O	R	I	D	H	E	E	P	U	V
U	Y	T	S	E	C	O	N	D	E
R	M	O	N	F	E	S	B	A	N

1. Jugendliche – ______________
2. Teelöffel – ______________
3. Rezept – ______________
4. Koch – ______________
5. Mehl – ______________
6. Backofen – ______________
7. Stück – ______________
8. Sekunde – ______________

12 Write the verbs.

1. kochen Do you often ______________ at home?
2. werden I want to ______________ a chef.
3. vorziehen Do you ______________ meat or fish?
4. schneiden Be careful! Don't ______________ yourself!

13 Match the sentence parts.

1. My mum twisted — a) of cake.
2. We're eating scrambled — b) yourselves!
3. Can you pass — c) the salt, please?
4. I'd like a piece — d) eggs.
5. Help — e) her ankle last week.

14 Write words for nice and not nice.

(Very) nice  Not nice 

(Very) nice	Not nice
good, delicious, ________	________
________	________
________	________

15 Find the words and complete the sentences.

We love ________ food. We eat it about once ________

and we often get a ________ from the restaurant.

We have a ________ with their menu so we can ________ by

phone. We also have a recipe book with our favourite ________ .

●16 Write the words and find the salad sauce.

1. A colourful cheese? _ _ _ ☐ _ _ _ _ _ _
2. Carry your dinner on this. _ _ _ ☐
3. It's a yellow fruit. _ _ ☐ _ _
4. Eat this as a main course with cheese and ham or with sugar as a dessert. _ _ ☐ _ _ _ _
5. A spicy yellow sauce. Eat it with sausages. _ _ _ _ ☐ _ _
6. It's a meat or a young sheep. _ ☐ _ _
7. It has vegetables and/or meat inside. It's not a wrap or a pie! _ _ _ ☐ _ _ _ _ _ _
8. An Italian dish! It's made of pasta, meat and cheese sauce. _ _ _ _ _ ☐ _
9. It's made with cheese and sugar. Eat it for dessert. _ _ _ _ ☐ _ _ _ _ _
10. A spoon for a drink? _ _ _ _ _ ☐ _ _

A white sauce for salads? _ _ _ _ _ _ _ _ _ _

●17 Find more food words.

1. wastr ____________
2. lowb ____________
3. massakou ____________
4. thickpoot ____________

●18 Find the right words.

1. He's the head ____________ .
2. She's at catering ____________ .
3. He's a friend of ____________ .
4. Can I have an entry ____________ , please?
5. Did you make that by ____________ ?

●19 Match the parts.

1. stir — a) some advice
2. add — b) the soup
3. give me — c) a pinch of salt

●20 Find and write five adjectives.

1. stolz ____________
2. geheim ____________
3. magisch ____________
4. super ____________
5. hart ____________

D	S	E	C	R	E	T
X	U	B	J	G	O	L
F	P	R	O	U	D	I
O	E	O	H	A	R	D
N	R	P	L	G	E	C
M	A	G	I	C	T	Y

Unit 5 In the news

Way in

p. 88	**TTYL (Talk to you later!)** ['tɔ:k tə ju ˌleɪtə]	Wir reden später!
	Good morning. [ˌgʊd 'mɔ:nɪŋ]	Guten Morgen.
	gamer ['geɪmə]	Spieler; Spielerin *(Computer)*
	to **stand** [stænd], **stood** [stʊd], **stood** [stʊd]	stehen
p. 89	to **travel** ['trævl]	reisen
	through [θru:]	durch
	fantasy ['fæntəsi]	Fantasie; Fantasy
	treasure ['treʒə]	Schatz
p. 88	**newspaper** ['nju:sˌpeɪpə]	Zeitung
	advertisement [əd'vɜ:tɪsmənt]	Anzeige; Werbespot
	text message ['tekst ˌmesɪdʒ]	SMS
	caller ['kɔ:lə]	Anrufer; Anruferin
p. 89	**LOL (Laugh out loud!)** ['lɑ:f aʊt ˌlaʊd]	Laut lachen!
	to **laugh** [lɑ:f]	lachen
	kiss [kɪs]	Kuss

Station 1

Media

to **chat** [tʃæt]	chatten; plaudern
online [ˌɒn'laɪn]	online
to **surf the internet** [ˌsɜ:f ði 'ɪntənet]	im Internet surfen
to **download** [ˌdaʊn'ləʊd]	herunterladen
to **upload** ['ʌpləʊd]	ins Internet stellen; hochladen
to **bookmark** ['bʊkmɑ:k]	zu … hinfügen

to copy ['kɒpi]	kopieren
to paste [peɪst]	einfügen
to save [seɪv]	speichern
file [faɪl]	Datei
text [tekst]	Text
video ['vɪdiəʊ]	Video
comment ['kɒment]	Kommentar
software ['sɒftweə]	Software

p. 90	**outside** [ˌaʊt'saɪd]	draußen; im Freien
	jacket ['dʒækɪt]	Jacke
	at the front of [ət ðə 'frʌnt‿əv]	an der Spitze (von); im vorderen Bereich
p. 92	to **take the dog for a walk** [ˌteɪk ðə ˌdɒg fər‿ə 'wɔ:k]	den Hund spazieren führen

Station 2

Activities

to **rap** [ræp]	rappen
to **try on** [ˌtraɪ 'ɒn]	anprobieren
to **hang (around)** [ˌhæŋ], **hung** [hʌŋ], **hung** [hʌŋ]	(herum)hängen
to **ride (a bike)** [ˌraɪd], **rode** [rəʊd], **ridden** ['rɪdn]	(Fahrrad) fahren
to **get dressed** [ˌget 'drest]	sich anziehen
to **repair** [rɪ'peə]	reparieren
to **talk to a neighbour** ['neɪbə]	mit dem Nachbar reden

	to have a haircut ['heəkʌt]	sich die Haare schneiden lassen
	to paint [peɪnt]	streichen; anmalen; malen
	to take a break [ˌteɪk‿ə 'breɪk]	Pause machen
p. 94	**moment** ['məʊmənt]	Moment; Augenblick
	while [waɪl]	während
	to **wave** [weɪv]	winken
p. 95	**in front of** [ɪn 'frʌnt‿əv]	vor; davor
p. 97	**I think so.** [aɪ 'θɪŋk səʊ]	Ich glaube.
	Your turn. [jɔ: 'tɜ:n]	Du bist dran.

Reading corner

p. 98	to **test** [test]	testen; prüfen
	roller coaster ['rəʊlə ˌkəʊstə]	Achterbahn
	ride [raɪd]	Fahrt; Ritt
	theme park ['θi:m ˌpɑ:k]	Freizeitpark; Themenpark
	billion ['bɪliən]	Milliarde
	to **fit** [fɪt]	passen
	island ['aɪlənd]	Insel
	to **be called** [bi: 'kɔ:ld]	heißen; genannt werden
p. 99	**South Pole** ['saʊθ ˌpəʊl]	Südpol
	to **ski** [ski:]	Ski fahren
	mile [maɪl]	Meile
	guide [gaɪd]	Führer; Führerin
	hard [hɑ:d]	schwer; schwierig
	to **swim** [swɪm], **swam** [swæm], **swum** [swʌm]	schwimmen
	way to go ['weɪ tə ˌgəʊ]	super
	America [ə'merɪkə]	Amerika
	texter ['tekstə]	SMS-Schreiber; SMS-Schreiberin
	text [tekst]	Text

	radio ['reɪdiəʊ]	Radio
	listener ['lɪsənə]	Zuhörer; Zuhörerin
	somebody else [ˌsʌmbədi 'els]	jemand anderes

Film corner

p. 101	**What about you?** [ˌwɒt‿əbaʊt 'juː]	Und du?
	to **agree** [ə'griː]	zustimmen
	to **disagree** [ˌdɪsə'griː]	anderer Meinung sein; nicht einverstanden sein
	I don't think so. [ˌaɪ dəʊnt 'θɪŋk səʊ]	Ich glaube nicht.
	part [pɑːt]	Teil

Writing skills

p. 106	**wall** [wɔːl]	Mauer; Wand
	out [aʊt]	heraus
	lettuce ['letɪs]	Kopfsalat
	finally ['faɪnli]	schließlich; zum Schluss
p. 107	**at last** [ət 'lɑːst]	endlich; zu guter Letzt

Verwende verschiedene Farben, um dir schwierige Wörter zu merken, z. B.:
gelb – die Aussprache fällt mir schwer
blau – die Rechtschreibung finde ich nicht so leicht
grün – die Bedeutung kann ich mir schlecht merken
Diese Wörter wiederholst du dann, bis du sie dir gut eingeprägt hast.

1 Write the text message.

2 Write the words.

1. A person who plays computer games.
2. You read this to find out what's new.
3. A person who calls a radio show.
4. Something you really want or like.
5. This is not real.
6. This makes you want to buy a thing.
7. Your mum may give you one of these.
8. You can write this on your mobile.

3 Match the words.

1. chat — a) a text message
2. surf — b) to music
3. write — c) online
4. read — d) the internet
5. listen — e) the newspaper

4 Complete the sentences.

a) Match the words.

try	hang	in front	on the
your	ride	turn	of
on	my bike	bus	around

b) Complete the sentences with the sentence parts from a).

1. I'd like to ________________ this jacket, please. – Yes, of course. Is that your size?

2. I ____________________ in the park and ________________ on Saturdays.

3. I met your brother ________________ yesterday. He was ________________ me and he was with a girl!

4. I cooked yesterday. So it's ________________ today.

5 Find the verbs. Write them next to the German.

1. lachen – ____________
2. reisen – ____________
3. stehen – ____________
4. plaudern – ____________
5. rappen – ____________
6. winken – ____________
7. (an)rufen – ____________

C	A	L	L	P
S	T	A	N	D
O	R	U	D	A
W	A	G	C	S
A	V	H	H	T
V	E	R	A	P
E	L	W	T	Y

6 Write the opposites.

1. here *there*
2. behind ____________
3. on the left ____________
4. first ____________

'Here' is the opposite of 'there'.

7 Write the words.

1. Augenblick ____________
2. während ____________
3. draußen ____________
4. Ich glaube. ____________
5. im vorderen Bereich ____________

8 Find the words.

▶ 1. You … at a funny joke.
4. It's music where you sing and talk at the same time.
5. A … is the title of a story in a newspaper.
6. She gives her mum a ….
8. Look on the internet; go ….
9. You can … down a mountain in winter.

▼ 2. A … shows you a tourist attraction.
3. A radio DJ talks to his … at home.
4. Can you write a … about the match?
7. I often … at the swimming pool.

9 Find the words and write them in the dialogue.

Bob: Did you buy that new game yesterday?

Helen: Yes, I bought it in the morning. ________________ ?

Bob: Oh, it was terrible. We didn't get to the shop until 4 p.m. and there were no more games there. We looked and looked and ________________ we found one under some boxes.

Helen: Did Janet get one too?

Bob: No, ________________ . She thinks it's a terrible game.

Helen: Oh, ________________ . I think it's great!

10 Write the words.

1. 

____

2. 
____

3. 
____

4. 
____

5. 
____

6. 
____

● 11 Complete the text with computer words.

I use the internet a lot. I d________________ songs and v__________ so that I can watch them on long trips. I often write a c_____________ about the videos I watch. I think that people like to read them. I download s______________ for my computer so I don't need to buy it in a shop.

I also find information for my homework on the internet. I copy it and s__________ it as a f__________ on my computer so that I can read the information again later. I NEVER c__________ and p__________ it into my homework, of course!

● 12 Write the verbs.

1. sich anziehen I _____________ after breakfast.
2. reparieren Can you _____________ my bike, please?
3. streichen I want to ___________ my bedroom green.
4. hochladen Don't __________ that photo on Facebook!
5. passen These books won't ___________ in my bag.
6. zustimmen Yes, I _____________ . It was a good film.

Unit 6 Goodbye Greenwich

Way in

p. 109	to **leave** [liːv], **left** [left], **left** [left]	abfahren; verlassen; lassen
	soon [suːn]	bald
	to **miss** [mɪs]	vermissen
	away [əˈweɪ]	weg; entfernt
	guys [gaɪz]	Leute
	Cornish [ˈkɔːnɪʃ]	Cornish; aus Cornwall
	smuggler [ˈsmʌglə]	Schmuggler; Schmugglerin
	the best [ðə ˈbest]	die besten
	baby [ˈbeɪbi]	Baby

Station 1

Holiday activities

to **make jewellery** [ˌmeɪk ˈdʒuːəlri]	Schmuck machen
to **go camping** [ˌgəʊ ˈkæmpɪŋ]	campen gehen; zelten
to **go beach combing** [gəʊ ˈbiːtʃ ˌkəʊmɪŋ]	den Strand nach Strandgut absuchen
to sleep in a tent [tent]	in einem Zelt schlafen
to surf on a big wave [sɜːf]	auf einer großen Welle surfen
to hike in the woods [ˌhaɪk ɪn ðə ˈwʊdz]	im Wald wandern gehen

p. 110	**plan** [plæn]	Plan
	three more days [ˌθriː mɔː ˈdeɪz]	noch drei Tage
	before [bɪˈfɔː]	*hier:* bis zu

	camp [kæmp]	Camp; Lager
	by the end [ˌbaɪ ði ˈend]	am Schluss
	jealous [ˈdʒeləs]	eifersüchtig; neidisch
	before [bɪˈfɔː]	vorher; zuvor
	leaving [ˈliːvɪŋ]	Abschieds-
p. 111	**table tennis** [ˈteɪbl ˌtenɪs]	Tischtennis
	to **look after** [ˌlʊk‿ˈɑːftə]	aufpassen; hüten
	slept [slept]	simple past, past participle von *to sleep* (schlafen)
	to **sell** [sel], **sold** [səʊld], **sold** [səʊld]	verkaufen
p. 113	**umbrella** [ʌmˈbrelə]	Regenschirm

Station 2

Farewell

farewell speech [feəˈwel spiːtʃ]	Abschiedsrede
to change school [ˌtʃeɪndʒ ˈskuːl]	die Schule wechseln
to pack up things [ˌpæk‿ʌp ˈθɪŋz]	Sachen packen
to say goodbye [ˈseɪ ˌɡʊdˈbaɪ]	sich verabschieden
to explore [ɪkˈsplɔː]	erkunden; erforschen
to feel at home quickly [ˌfiːl ət ˌhəʊm ˈkwɪkli]	sich schnell zu Hause fühlen
to have a new address [ˌhæv‿ə njuː əˈdres]	eine neue Adresse haben
to **keep in touch** [ˌkiːp ɪn ˈtʌtʃ]	in Verbindung bleiben
to **keep** [kiːp], **kept** [kept], **kept** [kept]	halten

p. 114	**flag** [flæɡ]	Flagge; Fahne
	scone [skɒn]	Scone *(eine Art süßes Brötchen)*

	Is something wrong? [ɪz 'sʌmθɪŋ rɒŋ]	Stimmt etwas nicht?
	a bit [ə 'bɪt]	ein bisschen; ein wenig
	to **have got** [hæv 'gɒt]	besitzen; haben
	silly ['sɪli]	albern
	forever [fə'revə]	für immer; ewig
p. 115	to **speak** [spi:k], **spoke** [spəʊk], **spoken** ['spəʊkn]	sprechen
	kind [kaɪnd]	freundlich; nett
p. 116	to **pack** [pæk]	packen; einpacken
	too much [ˌtu: 'mʌtʃ]	zu sehr
p. 117	**good luck** [ˌgʊd 'lʌk]	viel Glück

Reading corner

p. 118	**secret** ['si:krət]	Geheimnis
	cave [keɪv]	Höhle
	only ['əʊnli]	einzige
	strange [streɪndʒ]	merkwürdig; seltsam
	harbour ['hɑ:bə]	Hafen
	this way [ðɪs 'weɪ]	in diese Richtung
	rock [rɒk]	Fels; Stein
	to **watch** [wɒtʃ]	*hier:* beobachten
	funny ['fʌni]	merkwürdig; seltsam
p. 119	to **pick up** [ˌpɪk‿'ʌp]	aufheben
	stick [stɪk]	Stock
	now [naʊ]	heutzutage
	to **be scared** [bi: 'skeəd]	Angst haben; erschrocken sein
	against [ə'genst]	gegen
p. 118	**line** [laɪn]	Zeile; Linie

Film corner

p. 121	**inside** [ˌɪn'saɪd]	in … hinein
	ghost [gəʊst]	Geist
	to **scare** [skeə]	erschrecken

1 Write the words and find a place in England.

1. Things and people from Cornwall are … . ☐ _ _ _ _ _ ☐
2. Tomorrow is … . Next year is not. _ _ _ ☐
3. Long ago … lived in Cornwall. They brought things to England by boat. _ _ _ _ _ _ _ ☐ _
4. Cornwall is miles … from London. _ ☐ _ _
5. … is another word for people. "Well done, …!" ☐ _ _ _
6. What time do you … school? … is another word for "go away". _ ☐ _ _ _
7. My best friend moved to Australia last year and I still … her. _ ☐ _ _
8. I'm a United fan. They are … . _ _ _ _ _ ☐ _ _

The place in England is _ _ _ _ _ _ _ _ _ .

2 Write the words or phrases in English.

1. Plan — I have a good ______________ !
2. nach drei Tage — In ______________ it's my birthday.
3. Abschieds- — When is your ______________ party?
4. neidisch — He's got a new mobile. I'm ______________ .
5. am Schluss — ______________ of the day I was very tired.

3 Look at the pictures. Complete the sentences.

1. 

We often go ____________ .

2. 

We love to go

____________ .

3. 

We need my ____________ .

4. 

She's making ____________ .

5. 

We often

____________ .

6. 

I often ____________
my brother.

4 Match the words and write the sentences.

1. Is something	much!	____________
2. It's my farewell	wrong?	____________
3. Good	bit?	____________
4. Don't eat too	luck!	____________
5. Would you like a	speech.	____________

5 Complete the table.

Infinitive	Simple past	Pres. perfect (has/have ...)	German (Infinitive)
1. ______	______	______	zustimmen
2. leave	______	______	______
3. ______	missed	______	______
4. ______	______	spoken	______
5. ______	______	______	stehen
6. wave	______	______	______

6 Describe the people.

a) Find the words.

dink | lilsy | souljea | sirhytt | shefr | qicku

b) Match the words from a) with the right person or thing.

1. Joe is nice. He often does things for other people.

   He's ______________ .

2. Rob often does crazy things. He never thinks.

   He's ______________ .

3. Mike's girlfriend likes another boy.

   He's ______________ .

4. Mary went on a long walk. Now she needs a drink.

   She's ______________ .

5. These apples were on the tree a minute ago.

   They're ______________ .

6. Aysha always finishes her work in a minute.

   She's ______________ .

7 Write the words in English.

1. alle ______________________
2. haben ______________________
3. ewig ______________________

8 Match the sentence parts.

1. Let's go this — a) scared.
2. Don't pick — b) way.
3. I'm not — c) touch.
4. Let's keep in — d) up that stick.

9 Write the words in English and German.

1.  ______________________ ______________________
2.  ______________________ ______________________
3.  ______________________ ______________________
4.  ______________________ ______________________
5.  ______________________ ______________________
6.  ______________________ ______________________

10 Find 12 words. Write them next to the German.

S	T	R	A	N	G	E	O	U	P
E	A	I	G	L	Z	F	T	M	R
C	S	C	A	R	E	Q	O	B	D
R	Y	L	I	B	E	F	O	R	E
E	F	I	N	S	I	D	E	E	W
T	L	N	S	C	O	N	E	L	N
Y	A	E	T	Y	S	I	L	L	Y
S	G	G	H	O	S	T	I	A	M

1. Fahne ______________
2. Geist ______________
3. Linie ______________
4. gegen ______________
5. albern ______________
6. bis zu ______________
7. ein süßes Brötchen ______________
8. Geheimnis ______________
9. seltsam ______________
10. Regenschirm ______________
11. in … hinein ______________
12. erschrecken ______________

● 11 Write the missing words.

We often go camping in Cornwall in the summer. We all love to sleep in a ____________ even when it rains. We spend the whole day ____________. We go to the beach if we can. We go beach ____________ and we love to surf on big ____________ when it's windy. When it rains, we hike in the ____________ and sometimes we ____________ old castles. Holidays are great in Cornwall but I didn't want to move there. Now I have to change ____________ and say ____________ to my friends. Next we must ____________ up our things and we'll have a new ____________. I may ____________ at home quickly but I think I'll miss my friends ____________.

● 12 Write the words.

1. Fels ____________
2. seltsam ____________
3. heutzutage ____________
4. Quietsch! ____________!
5. einzige ____________
6. verkaufen ____________

L

Unit 1

1 1. aunt, 2. fantastic, 3. visit, 4. hat, 5. present, 6. cricket
2 1. e), 2. d), 3. a), 4. f), 5. c), 6. b)
3 1. parents, 2. grandparents, 3. uncle, 4. grandfather, 5. cousins
4 ▶ 1. city, 3. before, 5. ball ▼ 1. car, 2. well, 4. end
5 1. surprised, 2. excited, 3. worried, 4. angry, 5. unhappy, 6. hungry
6 your, mine, hers, yours, my, his
7 1. eye, 2. stairs, 3. ball, 4. pocket, 5. bus stop, 6. phone
8 1. tomorrow, 2. tonight, 3. concert, 4. company, 5. score, 6. dinner, 7. suddenly, 8. pocket
9 1. enjoy, enjoyed, 2. borrow, borrowed, 3. bring, brought, 4. give, gave, 5. feel, felt, 6. happen, happened, 7. lend, lent, 8. lose, lost, 9. understand, understood, 10. get, got
10 1. on purpose, 2. is right, 3. Have you got, 4. all right, 5. stop it
11 ▼ 1. best, 2. scene, 3. wake, 4. polite
▶ 5. escalator, 6. queue
● 12 1. afraid, 2. relaxed, 3. glad, 4. nervous, 5. jealous, 6. confused
● 13 1. pack (a suitcase), 2. take photos, 3. climb (a mountain), 4. go on a trip, 5. sunbathe, 6. fly (to another country)
1. e), 2. d), 3. a), 4. b), 5. f), 6. c)

Unit 2

1 1. organised, jumble, player, stage, crowd, job, star
2 1. buy, bought, bought – kaufen, 2. do, did, done – tun, 3. go, went, gone – gehen, 4. hear, heard, heard – hören, 5. see, saw, seen – sehen, 6. take, took, taken – nehmen
3 1. He has done the shopping. 2. She has taken the rubbish out. 3. He has tidied his room. 4. She has cleaned her football boots. 5. He has texted his friend / Ken.
4 1. already, 2. just, 3. yet
5 Hi Luke, Where are you? You are late. The film has started. It's great. See you in the cinema or at my house tomorrow? Dave
6 1. boot, 2. interview, 3. website, 4. actor, 5. supermarket, 6. lines, 7. list, 8. flight
7 1. actor, 2. director, 3. hairdresser, 4. waiter, 5. singer, 6. doctor, 7. football player
8 1. forgotten, 2. been, 3. won, 4. made
9 ▼ 1. embarrassed, 4. nervous, 6. yet
▶ 2. amazing, 3. Spain, 5. forgotten, 7. ever, 8. young
10 1. 2 p.m., 2. 8 a.m., 3. 11:59 a.m., 4. 10:15 p.m.
11 1. child, 2. children, 3. (many) judge(s), 4. a / one lady
12 1. remember, 2. panic, 3. believe, 4. practise, 5. hurry
13 1. head, 2. nose, 3. mouth, 4. eye, 5. ear, 6. stomach, 7. arm, 8. leg, 9. foot
14 ache, sore, hurt, headache, tablets, ill
● 15 a) washing up, it, floor, cake, table, bottle bank, shopping, bottles, rubbish
b) done / washing up, taken / rubbish, made / cake, swept / floor, done / shopping, taken bottles / bottle bank, laid / table, eaten / it
● 16 1. nurse, 2. lorry driver, 3. builder, 4. shop assistant, 5. chef, 6. vet

Unit 3

1 city, boat trip, sights, big wheel, built, buildings, clock tower, royal, ago, prison, restaurant

2 1. UK, 2. France, 3. the Netherlands, 4. the Czech Republic, 5. Spain, 6. Australia, 7. Turkey

3 1. church – Kirche, 2. castle – Burg, 3. stadium – Stadion, 4. market – Markt, 5. bridge – Brücke, 6. taxi – Taxi, 7. bell – Glocke

4 1. one / a hundred and one, 2. five hundred and eighty-two, 3. three hundred and thirty-four, 4. three thousand and twenty-one, 5. nine thousand, two hundred and nineteen

5 1. London Eye: Height, weighs, tonnes, 2. Big Ben: high, bell, 3. St Paul's Cathedral: built, dome

6 1. office, 2. TV studio, 3. visitor, 4. sunbathe, 5. pretty, 6. fact

7 top, suits, isn't it, look for, size, shop assistant, these

8 1. dry – wet, trocken – nass, 2. terrible – fantastic, schrecklich – großartig, 3. long – short, lang – kurz, 4. low – high, niedrig – hoch, 5. cheap – expensive, billig – teuer, 6. young – old, jung – alt, 7. grey – colourful, grau – bunt

9 ▼ 1. passenger, 2. sunglasses, 4. real, 5. price
▶ 3. airport, 6. fly, 7. bargain, 8. each, 9. stickers

● 10 1. mosque, 2. lake, 3. monument, 4. square, 5. floor

● 11 1. loose, 2. unfashionable, 3. plain, 4. uncomfortable

● 12 on, fire, burnt down, luckily, brick

● 13 1. plank, 2. cannon, 3. cannon ball(s), 4. roof, 5. fire engine, 6. carpenter, 7. tools

● 14 1. boss, 2. across, 3. part, 4. as, 5. drama, 6. when

Unit 4

1 1. pie, 2. egg, 3. potato salad, 4. bread, 5. chicken, 6. coconut, 7. cheese, 8. rice, 9. sausage(s), 10. pasty, 11. salad, 12. vegetables, 13. potato(es), 14. cabbage, 15. carrot(s), 16. onion

2 grandma, Jamaican, spices, sort, delicious / yummy, made, Yummy / Delicious

3 1. choose, chose, chosen – auswählen, 2. spend, spent, spent – ausgeben, 3. fly, flew, flown – fliegen, 4. sound, sounded, sounded – klingen

4 1. starter, 2. main course, 3. dessert

5 1. packed lunch, 2. mashed potatoes, 3. apple crumble 4. pasta bake

6 usually, mashed potatoes, allergic, payment, quick

7 1. news, 2. many, 3. meal, 4. fried

8 ▶ 2. soup, 4. strawberry, 7. tomato, 9. pudding
▼ 1. custard, 2. spaghetti, 3. garlic, 5. beef, 6. ham, 8. onion

9 1. cup, 2. glass, 3. plate, 4. fork, 5. knife, 6. spoon

10 2. plantain – Kochbanane, 3. wrap – Wrap, 4. napkin – Serviette, 5. combination – Kombination, 6. menu – Speisekarte, 7. thirsty – durstig, 8. order – bestellen

11 1. teen, 2. teaspoon, 3. recipe, 4. chef, 5. flour, 6. oven, 7. piece, 8. second

12 1. cook, 2. become, 3. prefer, 4. cut

13 1. e), 2. d), 3. c), 4. a), 5. b)

14 ☺ lovely, beautiful, pretty, fantastic, brilliant, great, cute
☹ awful, bad, terrible

15 Indian, a week, takeaway, flyer, order, dishes

● 16 1. blue cheese, 2. tray, 3. lemon, 4. pancake, 5. mustard, 6. lamb, 7. spring roll, 8. lasagne, 9. cheesecake, 10. teaspoon; MAYONNAISE

● 17 1. straw, 2. bowl, 3. moussaka, 4. toothpick

● 18 1. chef, 2. college, 3. mine, 4. form, 5. yourself

● 19 1. b), 2. c), 3. a)

● 20 1. proud, 2. secret, 3. magic, 4. super, 5. hard

Unit 5

1 Hi Mike, Where are you? You are missing a great football match. Laugh out loud! We're losing. Talk to you later. See you tomorrow. Tina

2 1. gamer, 2. newspaper, 3. caller, 4. treasure, 5. fantasy, 6. advertisement, 7. kiss, 8. text message

3 1. c), 2. d), 3. a), 4. e), 5. b)

4 1. try on, 2. hang around, ride my bike, 3. on the bus, in front of, 4. your turn

5 1. laugh, 2. travel, 3. stand, 4. chat, 5. rap, 6. wave, 7. call

6 2. in front of, 3. on the right, 4. last

7 1. moment, 2. while, 3. outside, 4. I think so. 5. at the front of

8 ▶ 1. laugh, 4. rap, 5. headline, 6. kiss, 8. online, 9. ski
▼ 2. guide, 3. listeners, 4. report, 7. swim

9 What about you, at last, I don't think so, I disagree

10 1. newspaper, 2. jacket, 3. roller coaster, 4. island, 5. wall, 6. lettuce

● 11 download, videos, comment, software, save, file, copy, paste

● 12 1. get dressed, 2. repair, 3. paint, 4. upload, 5. fit, 6. agree

Unit 6

1 1. Cornish, 2. soon, 3. smugglers, 4. away, 5. guys, 6. leave, 7. miss, 8. the best; GREENWICH

2 1. plan, 2. three more days, 3. leaving, 4. jealous, 5. By the end

3 1. camping, 2. beach combing, 3. umbrella, 4. jewellery, 5. play table tennis, 6. look after

4 1. Is something wrong? 2. It's my farewell speech. 3. Good luck! 4. Don't eat too much! 5. Would you like a bit?

5 1. agree, agreed, agreed – zustimmen, 2. leave, left, left – verlassen, 3. miss, missed, missed – vermissen, 4. speak, spoke, spoken – sprechen, 5. stand, stood, stood – stehen, 6. wave, waved, waved – winken

6 a) kind, silly, jealous, thirsty, fresh, quick
b) 1. Joe – kind, 2. Rob – silly, 3. Mike – jealous, 4. Mary – thirsty, 5. apples – fresh, 6. Aysha – quick

7 1. all, 2. have got, 3. forever

8 1. b), 2. d), 3. a), 4. c)

9 1. cave – Höhle, 2. stick – Stock, 3. harbour – Hafen, 4. ghost – Geist, 5. mountain – Berg, 6. sunglasses – Sonnenbrille

10 1. flag, 2. ghost, 3. line, 4. against, 5. silly, 6. before, 7. scone, 8. secret, 9. strange, 10. umbrella, 11. inside, 12. scare

● 11 tent, outside, combing, waves, woods, explore, school, goodbye, pack, address, feel, forever

● 12 1. rock, 2. funny / strange, 3. now, 4. Creak! 5. only, 6. sell

Arbeitsanweisungen mit Operatoren

Complete the sentences • the dialogue • the text • the table.
Vervollständige die Sätze • den Dialog • den Text • die Tabelle.

Describe the people • the picture(s).
Beschreibe die Menschen • das Bild/die Bilder.

Find the words • the verbs • the pairs • the phrases • the activities and write them (down).
Finde die Wörter • die Verben • die Paare • die Satzteile • die Aktivitäten und schreibe sie auf.

Find the wrong word.
Finde das falsche Wort.

Look at the pictures.
Schau dir die Bilder an.

Match the words • the (sentence) parts.
Ordne die Wörter • die Satzteile zu.

Make sentences.
Bilde Sätze.

Put in the right verb • the right form of the verb.
Setze das richtige Verb • die richtige Form des Verbs ein.

Write the (missing) words • numbers • the phrases in English.
Schreibe die (fehlenden) Wörter • Nummern • Satzteile auf Englisch auf.

Write the right word • the opposites.
Schreibe das richtige Wort • die Gegenteile auf.

Write the words next to the German.
Schreibe die Wörter neben das Deutsche.

Notizen